ADULT COLO

MW01443121

cyberpunk

Craft Genius
BOOKS

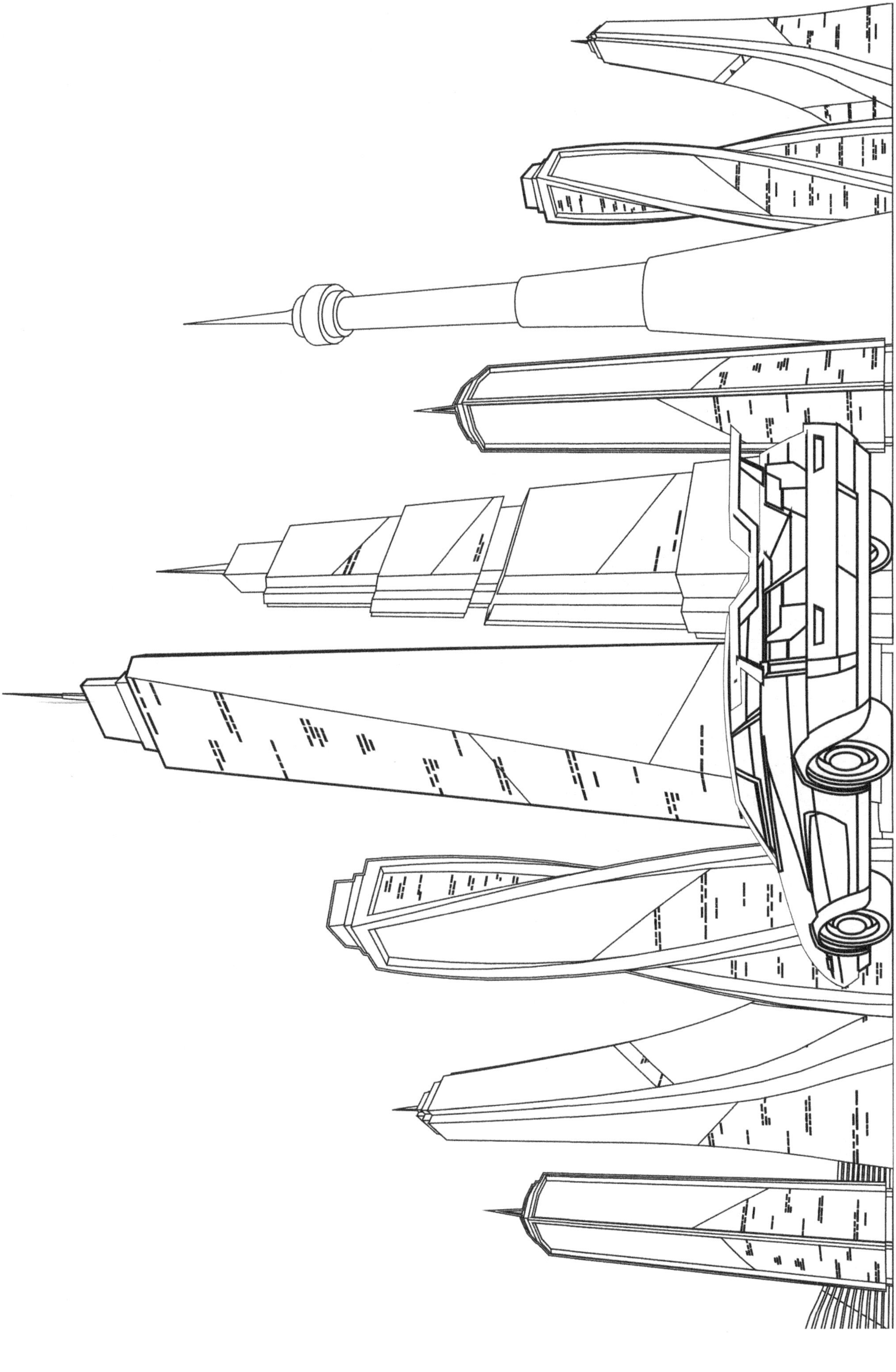

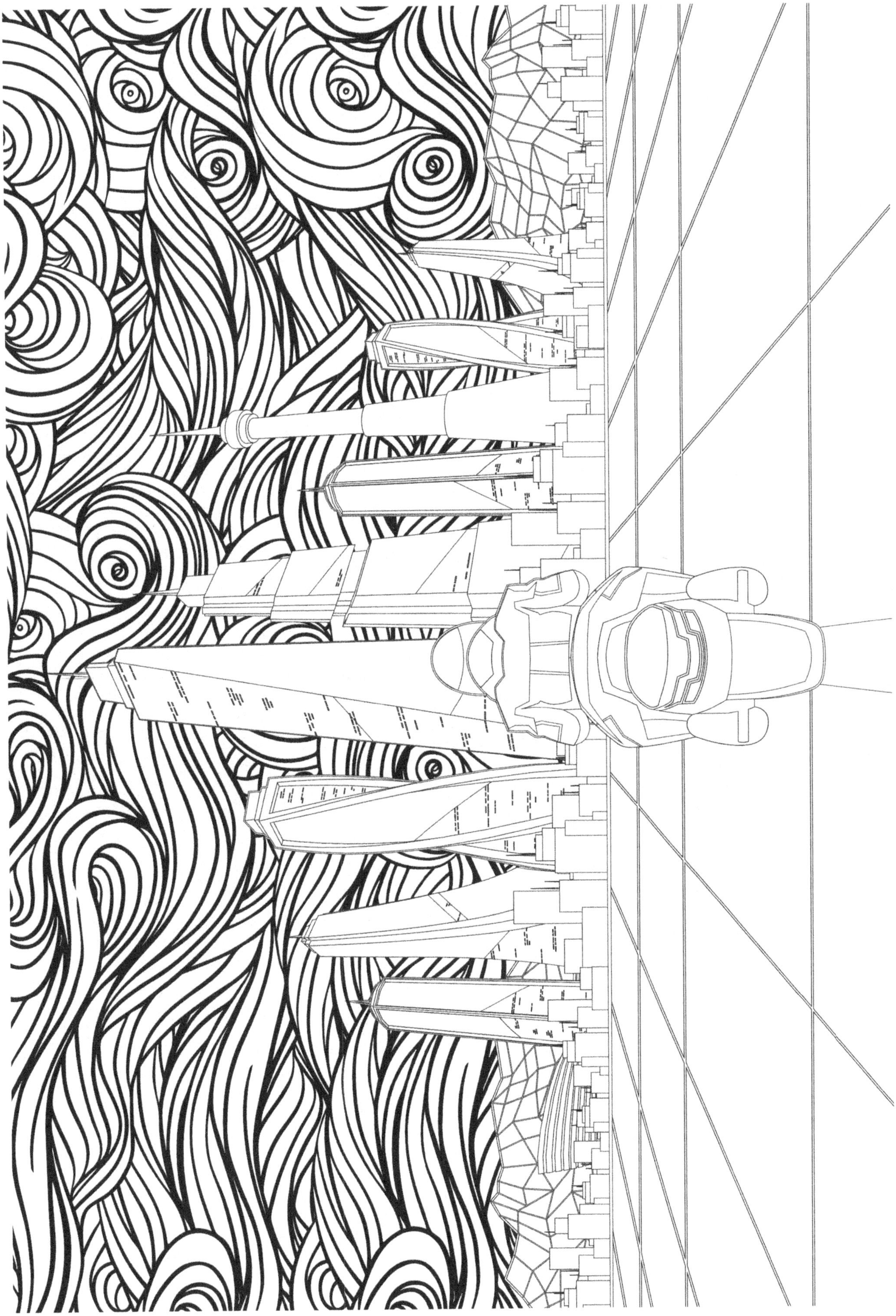

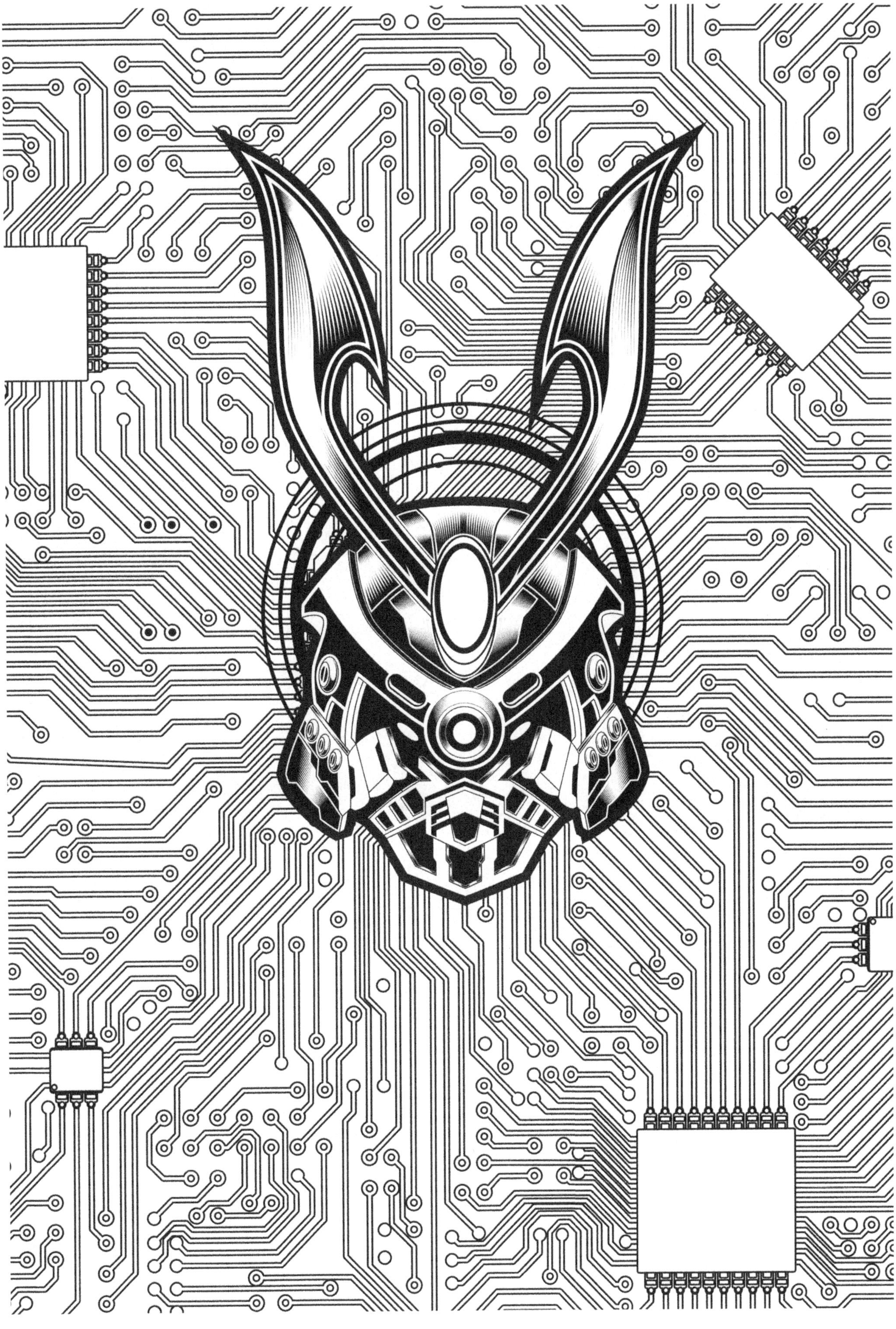

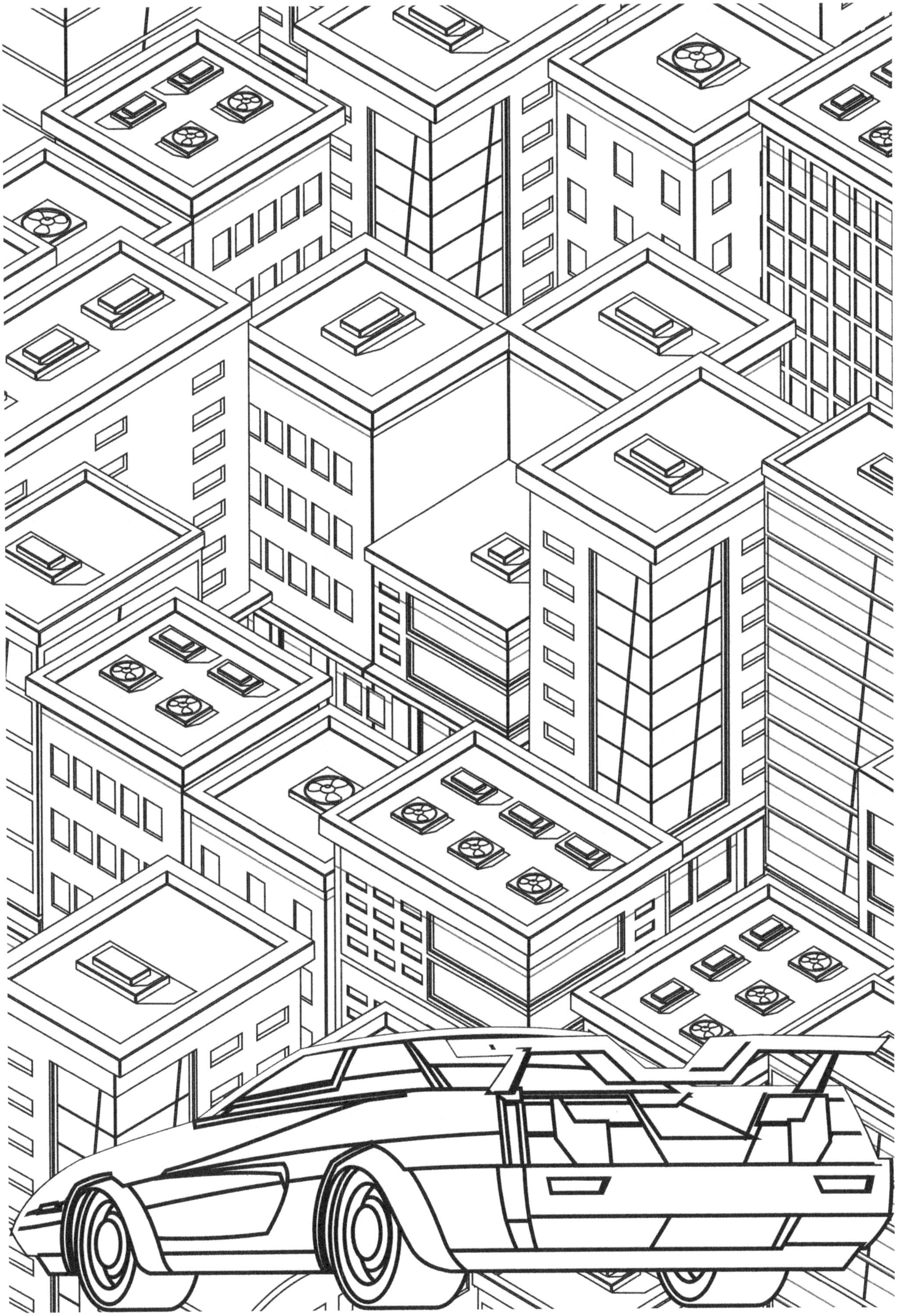

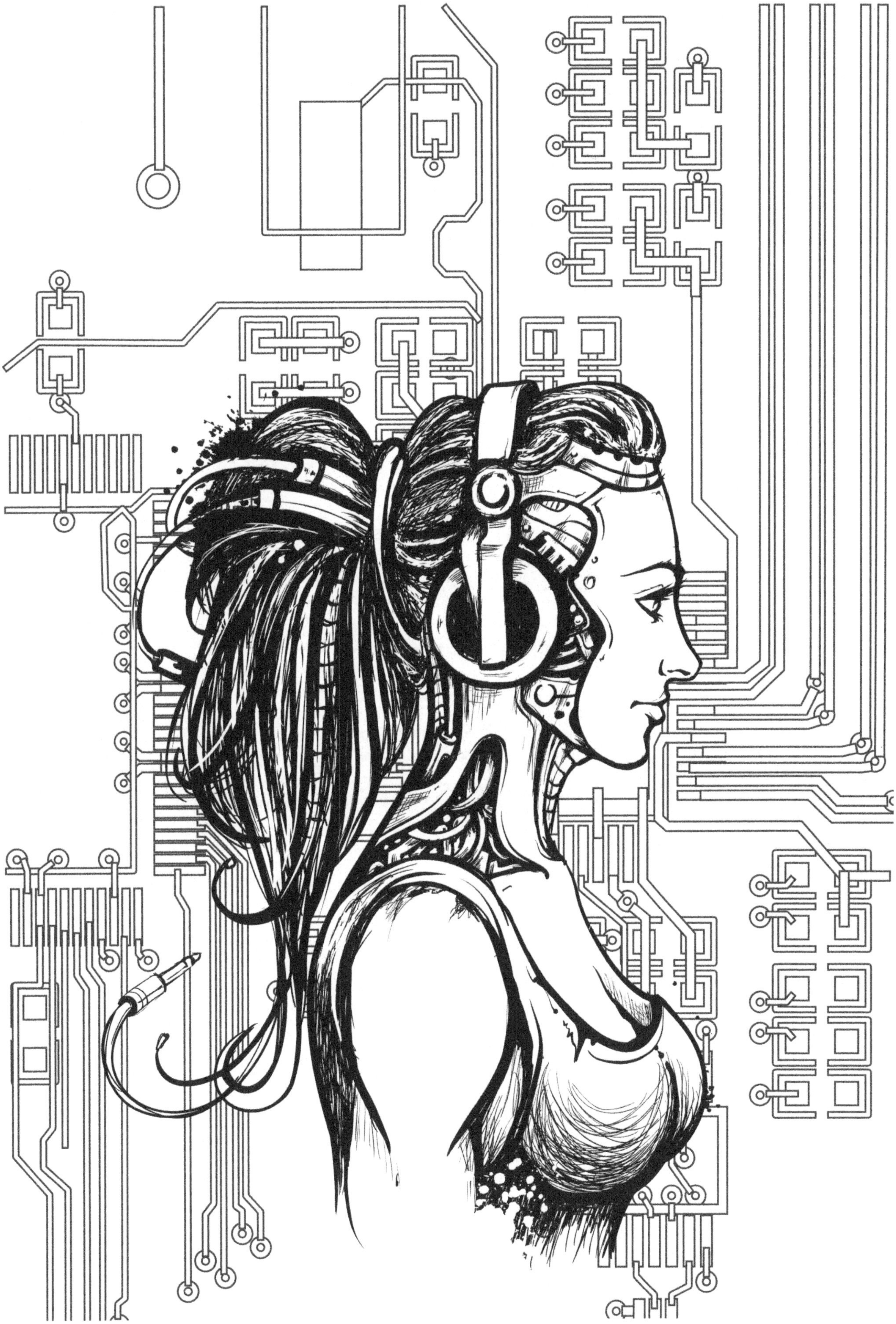

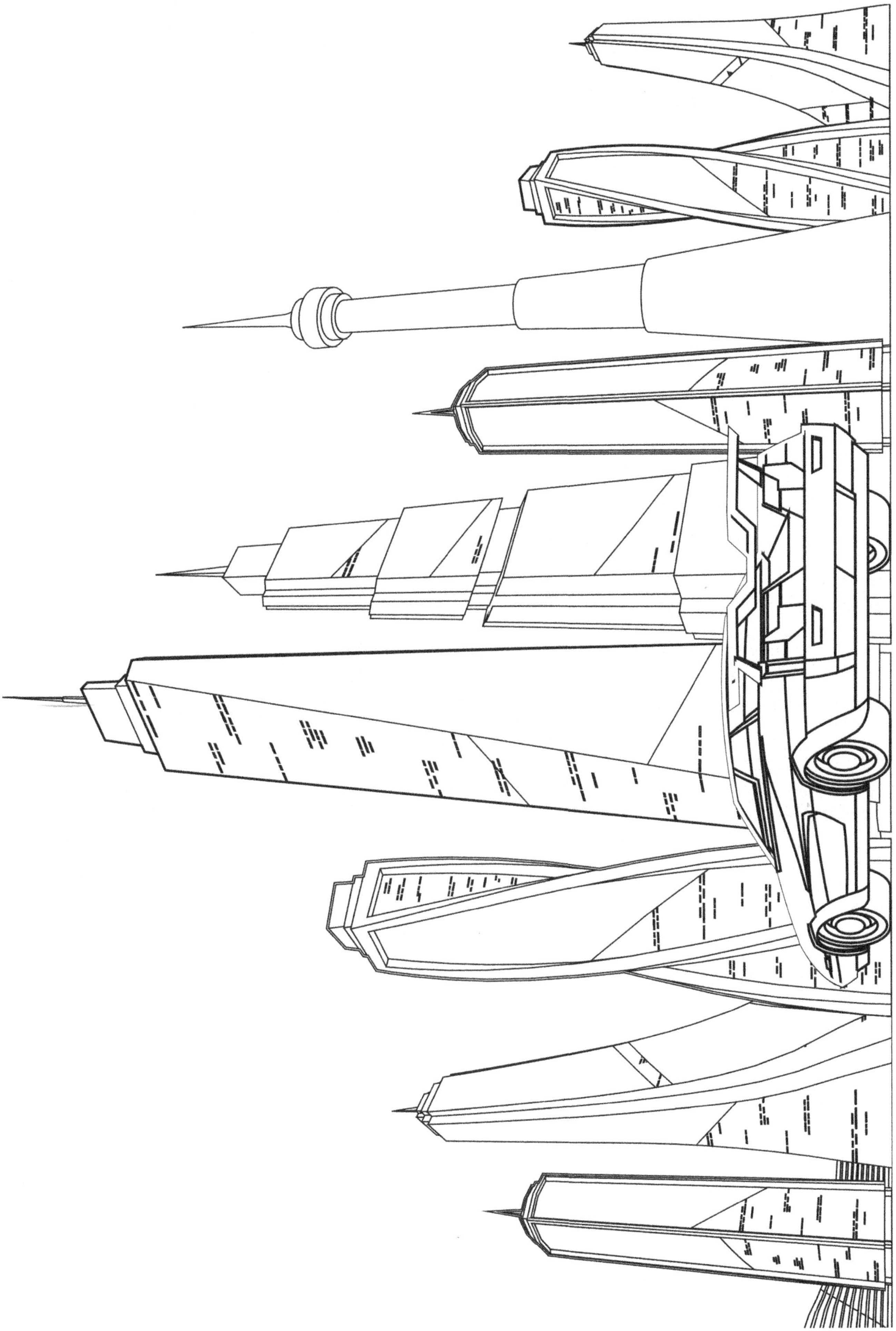

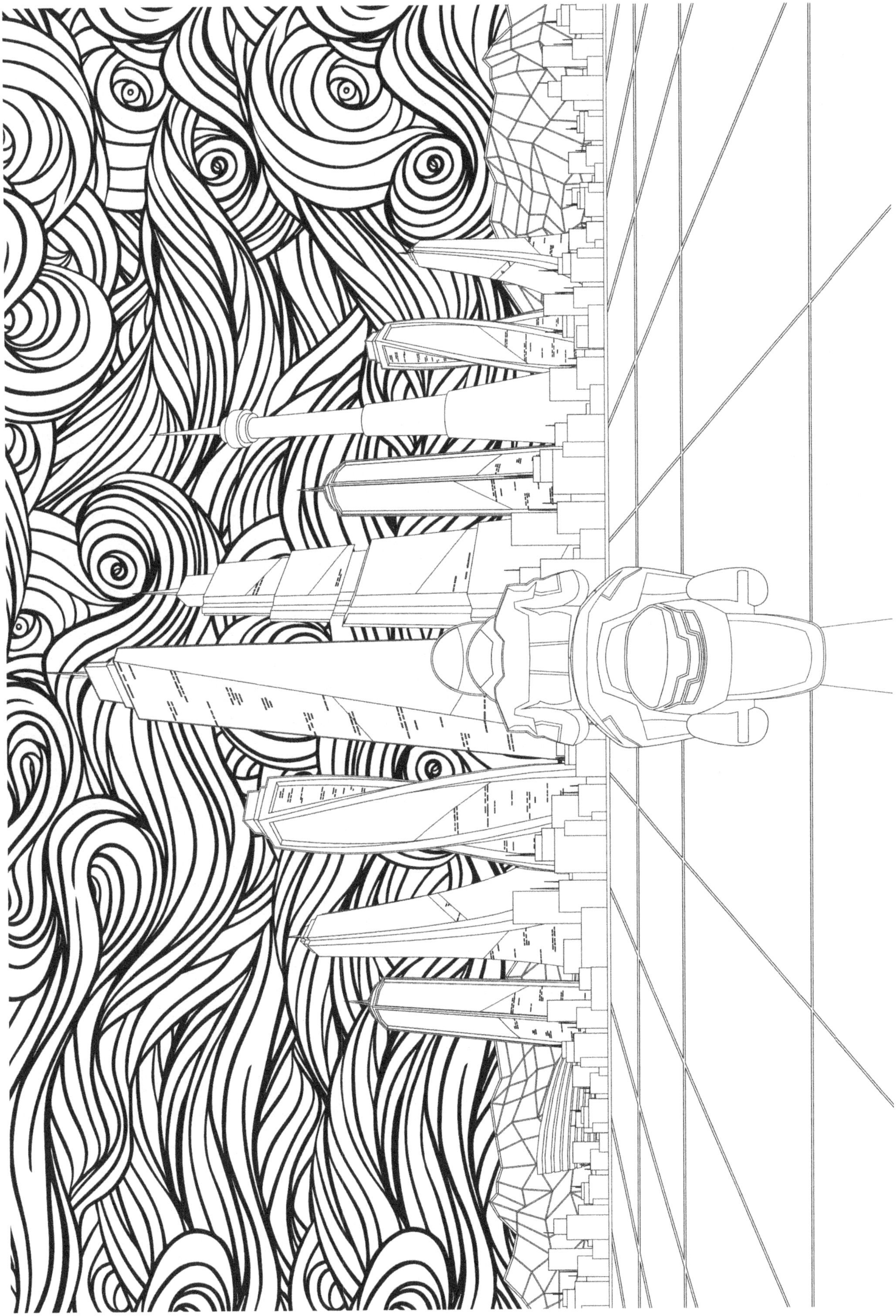

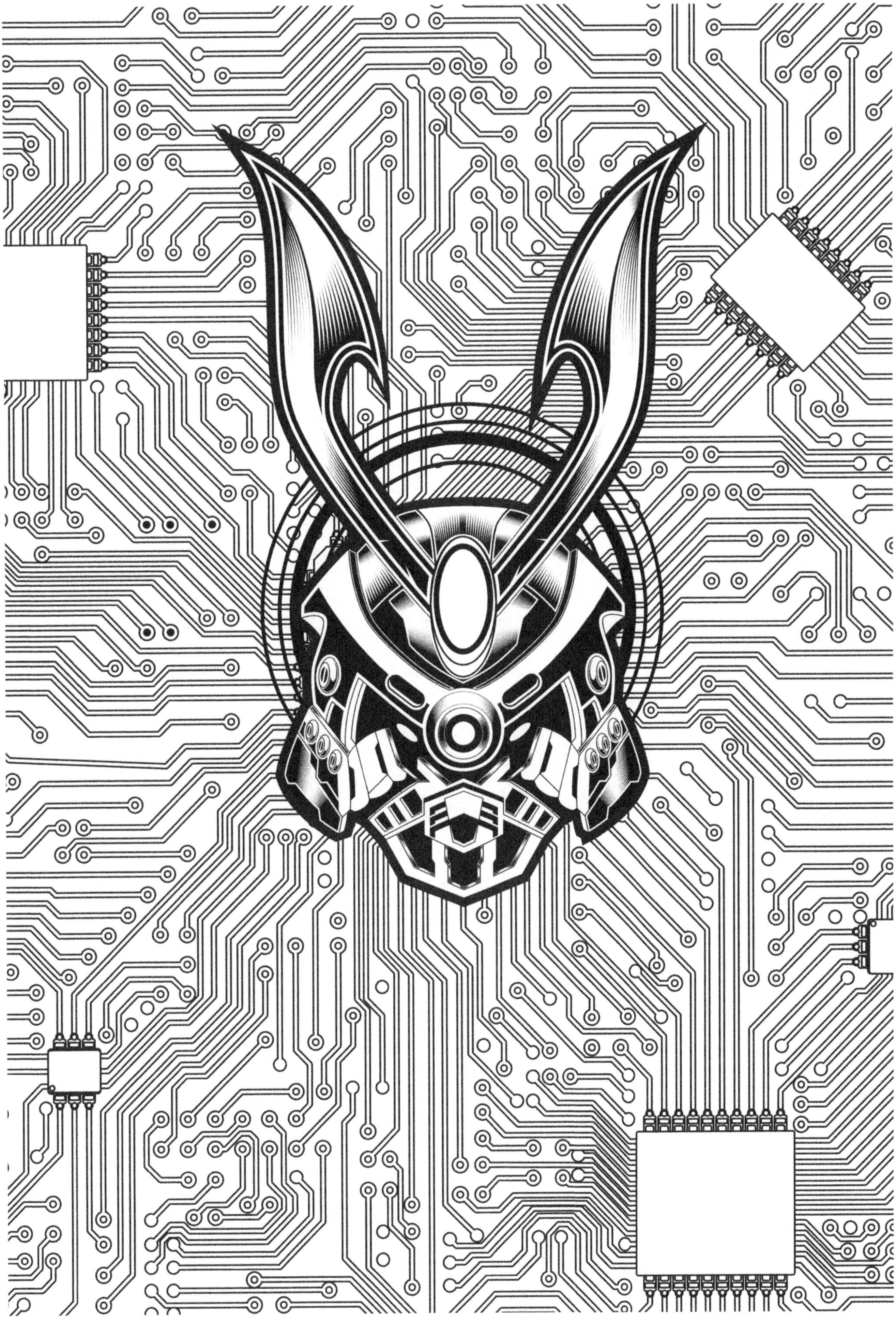

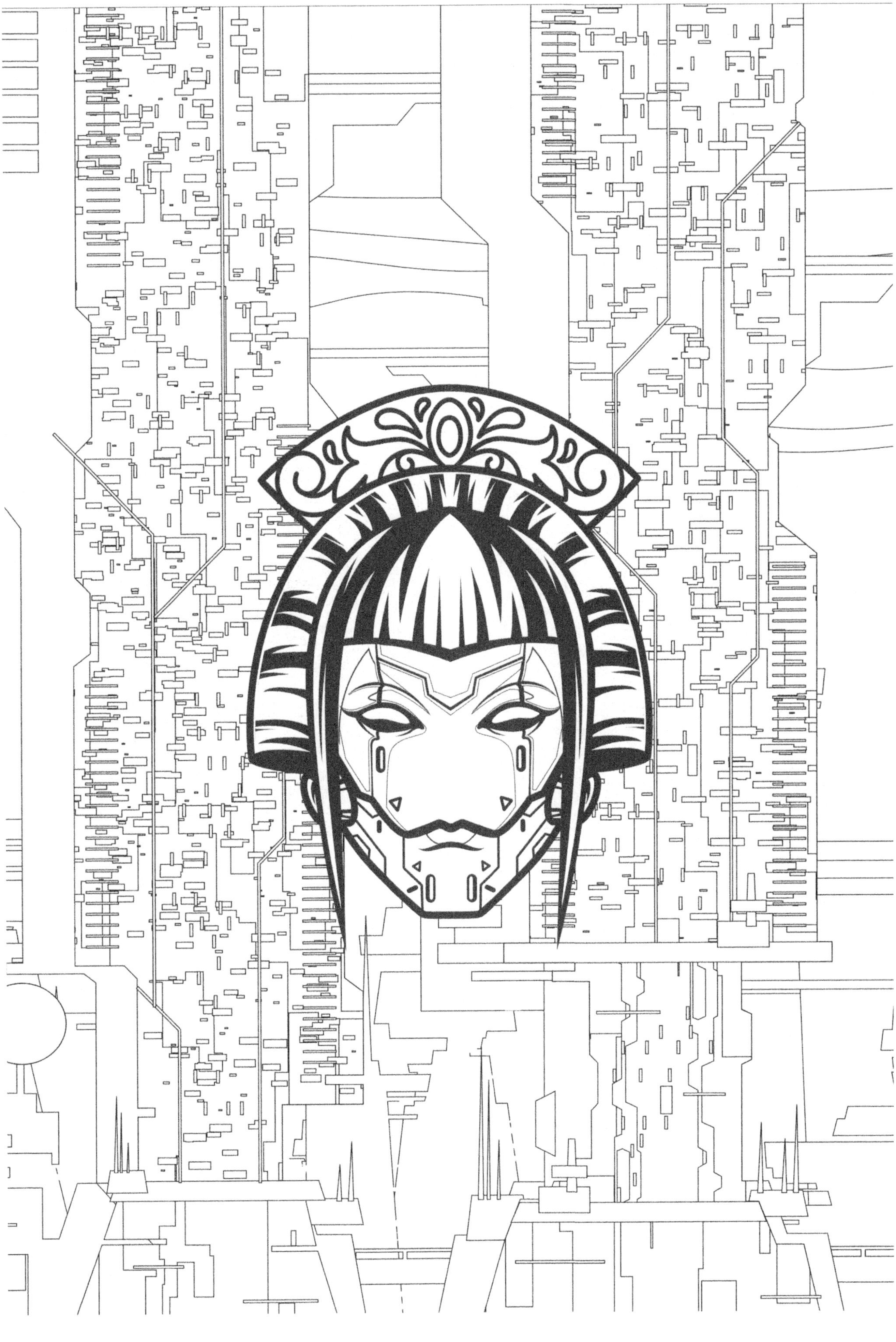

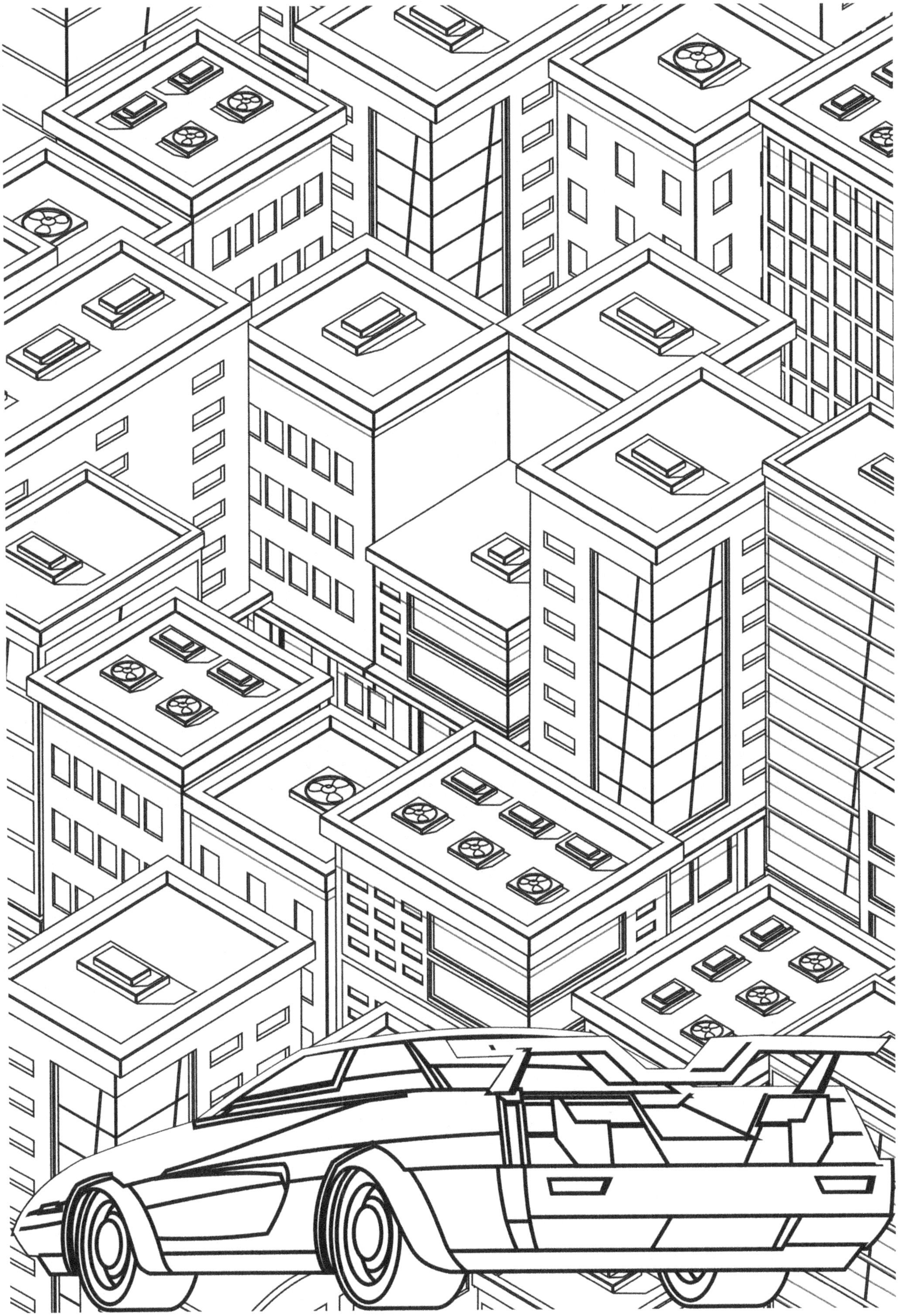

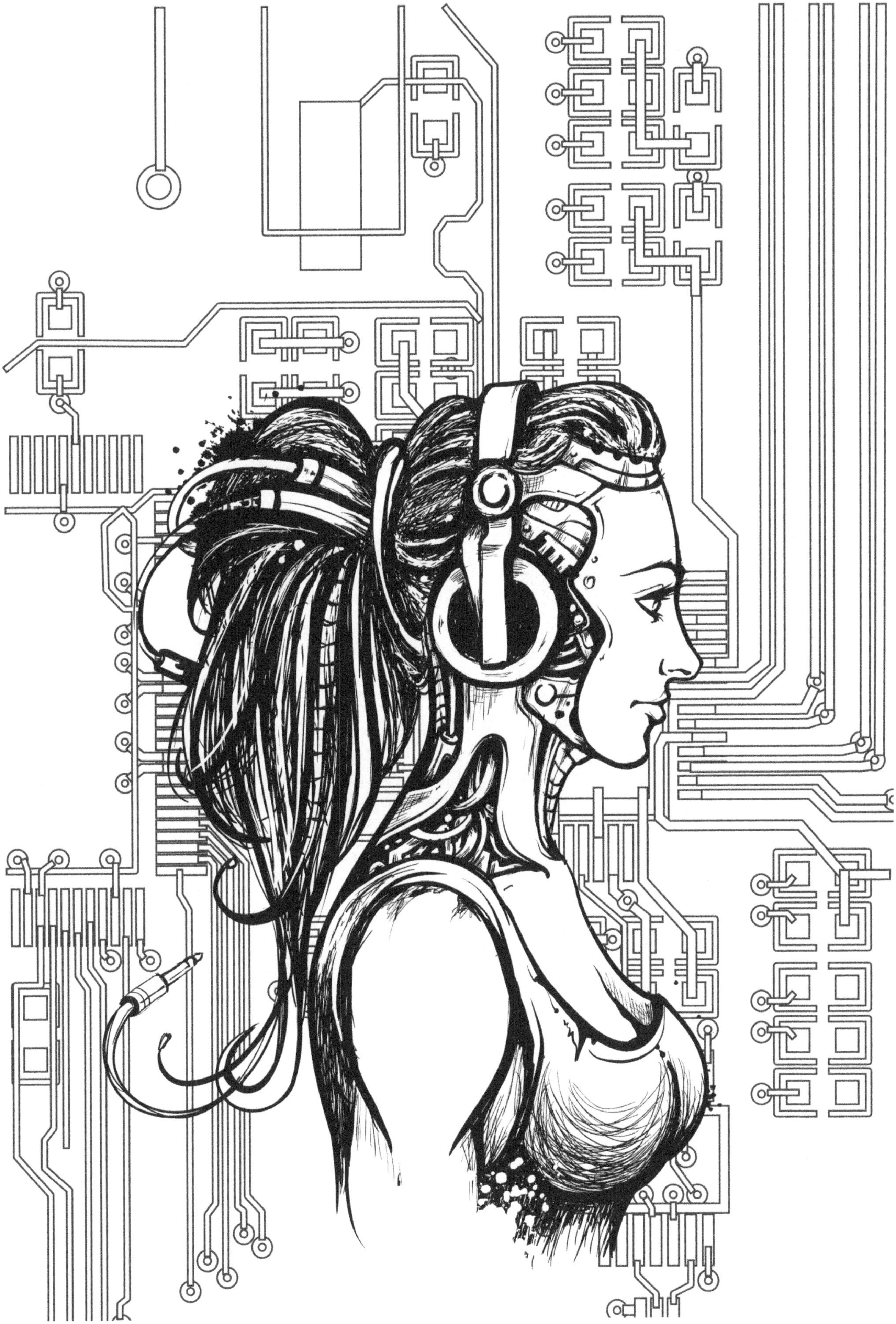